FAMOUS SKULLS

"It's funny the way people love the dead.
Once you are dead, you are made for life."
— Jimi Hendrix

ISBN-13: 978-1719369558

ISBN-10: 1719369550

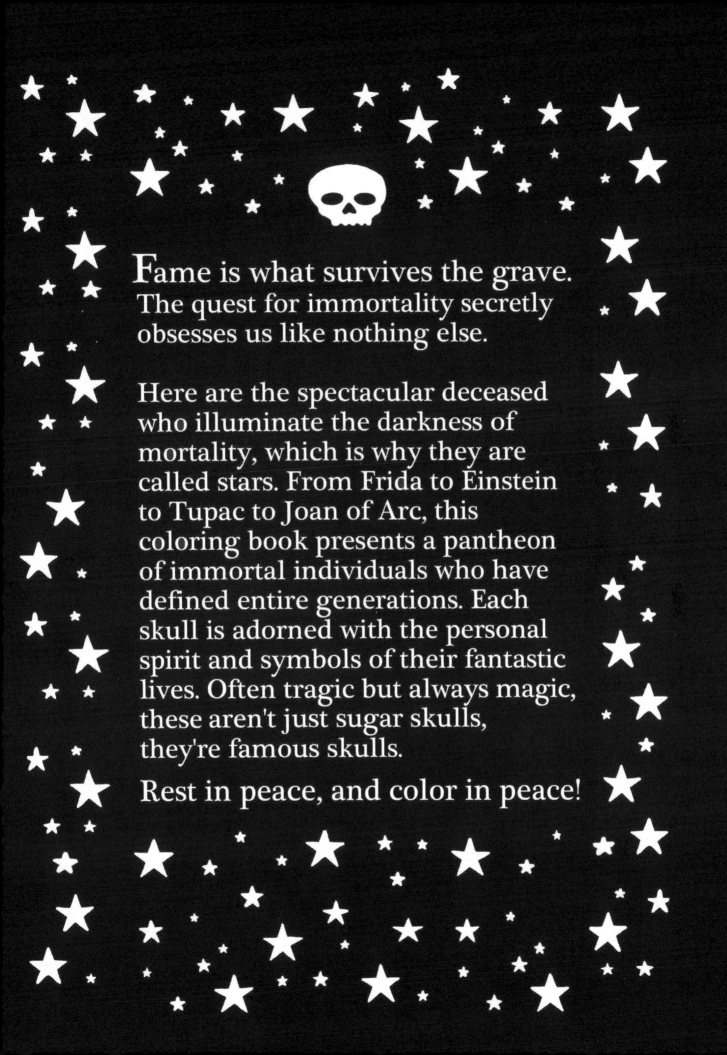

Fame is what survives the grave. The quest for immortality secretly obsesses us like nothing else.

Here are the spectacular deceased who illuminate the darkness of mortality, which is why they are called stars. From Frida to Einstein to Tupac to Joan of Arc, this coloring book presents a pantheon of immortal individuals who have defined entire generations. Each skull is adorned with the personal spirit and symbols of their fantastic lives. Often tragic but always magic, these aren't just sugar skulls, they're famous skulls.

Rest in peace, and color in peace!

her parrots & monkeys cry & shout
she paints her last portrait in her blue house
the most famous of all unibrows
now her colors will never go out
& with that garden upon her head
she brings new life to the land of the dead
the artist of her own paradise
ascending on the wings of a perfect butterfly . . .

" I paint flowers so they will not die. "
— Frida Kahlo

he blazed through life
& raced on nighttime streets
a rebel on the silver screen
west of hollywood & east of eden
but alas there is no unscathed immortality
for even a giant can perish & bleed
though his fame & spirit shall never fade . . .

" Dream as if you'll live forever.
Live as if you'll die today. "
— James Dean

the face that launched a thousand pictures
eternal representation of a beautiful victim
that sensual smile
those flowing clothes
& all of it captured in each movie role
but beyond the glamorous symbol
they did not care to know
for here was a puzzle in pieces
only wanting to be whole ...

" Hollywood is a place where they'll pay you
a thousand dollars for a kiss
and fifty cents for your soul. "
— Marilyn Monroe

with a mind given to the morbid
his life was a sad short story
loved ones died but he survived
so from a broken soul he writes
of ravens tapping at the door
& hearts beating beneath the floor
nevermore nevermore
edgar poe edgar poe
of a health so desperate & poor
until his last breath is taken in baltimore
oh the tragedy of women & men
blacker than the ink upon his pen . . .

" The boundaries which divide Life from Death
are at best shadowy and vague.
Who shall say where one ends,
and where the other begins? "
— Edgar Allan Poe

the thrilling disguise of a worldwide idol
but what the media image hides
is a childhood unravelled
a prodigy always performing
& forever scrutinized
bad & beat it & billy jean
all the fans & success
but never any peace of mind
was it worth the sacrifice
the cost of all those burning lights ...

" A star can never die.
It just turns into a smile
and melts back into the cosmic music,
the dance of life. "
— Michael Jackson

one of the most esteemed paintings in history
leonardo da vinci's masterpiece
a femme fatale shrouded in mystery
her real name was lisa del giocondo
a noblewoman from florence italy
& she who's been dead for quite a while
continues to seduce the world with her smile . . .

" Just to get a glance at me,
they stand in line for miles. "
— Mona Lisa

* not a real quote, she never left behind any

the dirt blows in from the west
& they do not see him pass
a man in black
walking a barren land
with a silver guitar in hand
he's preachin' sin & revelation
he's singin' ruin & redemption
rings of fire & jacob's ladder
his time has come at last
he's witnessing the ultimate judgement
of slave & master
the everlasting rapture of god's plan . . .

" How well I have learned that there
is no fence to sit on between heaven and hell.
There is a deep, wide gulf, a chasm, and that
chasm is no place for any man. "
— Johnny Cash

during the revolutionary war
he crossed the icy delaware
then at the battle of yorktown
the british finally broke down
independence was secured
& a legend was born
here was
the first president of liberty's realm
the man on the dollar bill
skillful general & a nation's father . . .

" If the freedom of speech is taken away
then dumb and silent we may be led,
like sheep to the slaughter. "
— George Washington

here was a king with no jeweled crown
leading his people out of jim crow's bounds
the civil disobedience that held back a storm
& changed the backward tides of an entire nation
for they who heard his sunlit revelation
could no longer accept the darkness of segregation
an exodus from montgomery to washington d.c.
that only stopped
when he was shot
in memphis tennessee
but no evil or conspiracy
shall ever stop the march for freedom & peace ...

" I have a dream. "
— Martin Luther King

cry of love
guitar on fire
he conjures the gods
of rock & desire
higher & higher
until he kisses the sky
but everything that goes up must surely fall
especially when the drugs take control
guitar in pieces
now he rests in a field of purple flowers
& as they gather all along the watchtower
this is what the joker tells the thief
the body always dies
but the other replies
yes but the soul's released . . .

" When the power of love
overcomes the love of power
the world will know peace. "
— Jimi Hendrix

he was short not tall
a sickly boy from the island of corsica
but he who was so physically flawed
would one day rise to conquer the world
from a poor lowly artilleryman
he became emperor of the french
& after the battle of austerlitz
all of europe was almost his
he thought his star would never set
but marching against the russians
was the beginning of the end
the british quickly pursued
& at the battle of waterloo
he finally met his doom
dying on a dungeon island
he who broke all the rules
now regrets the world he almost ruled ...

" Impossible is a word to be found
only in the dictionary of fools. "
— Napoleon Bonaparte

to make our world peaceful
was the burning mission of this beatle
for even as the hawk feeds on the dove
he knew that hatred could not defeat love
no repeat of vietnam
or president nixon
no insane government
or crazy man with a gun
shall ever kill off what he imagined
the enduring message of his songs
for somewhere over the rainbow
we will one day reap what we sow . . .

" Love is the flower you've got to let grow. "
— John Lennon

a vision of saints in the garden
would make her into france's savior & martyr
in her 13th year she heard the voice of god
this gave her the courage to end the 100 year's war
the church bells rang at the siege of orléans
she couldn't be defeated & the enemy retreats
until one day she was captured by the english
& on a stake they burnt her like a common witch
but the roaring flame
could not destroy the kindled faith
for everything about her was truly miraculous
& so her legend outlived death's kiss . . .

" I am not afraid ... I was born for this."
— Joan of Arc

fools rush in as the angels sing
they come to honor this electric king
his guitar & his dancing
like thunder & lightning
hound dogs cry
he didn't stay
so throw another one in the jukebox
& let his records play . . .

" Truth is like the sun.
You can shut it out for a time,
but it ain't goin' away. "
— Elvis Presley

in a fever dream
she remembers her younger years
living near a forest stream
with running wolves & standing bears
a chief's daughter with beads & feathers in her hair
now she walks between two worlds
a woman of nature dying in england's gloom
gone are the splendid days of tribal living
she passes into the night land of wild visions . . .

" All must die.
Tis' enough that the child liveth. "
— Pocahontas

all eyes on him
he was rap's revolution
calling for the ghetto's evolution
but within this angry proud soul
there battled armies of demons & angels
violent problems & peaceful solutions
bloody thorns on a concrete rose
dear mama & california love
the never-ending drama of a tormented thug
in las vegas he would die young
as he stared at the world through his review
a rain of bullets came through his window
losing blood beside the car's door
he could not fight the pain anymore
so behold
hip hop's eternal martyr . . .

" You know it's funny when it rains it pours.
They got money for wars,
but they can't feed the poor."
— Tupac Shakur

alas poor shakespeare i knew him well
a royal bard so poetically blessed
and
they who hath performed his plays a million times
have shown just why he remains the mirror of life
he gives a final bow & walks off stage
but beneath his writer's brow there rests
the scorn & delight of every age
comedy's hope & tragedy's crime
that infinite dance of darkness with light
hither is the mask that smiles
tither is the mask that cries
to be or not to be
a question mark for you & me
oh word weaver of forlorn doom
leaving us your riddles of burning beauty . . .

" Thou know'st 'tis common; all must die,
Passing through nature to eternity. "
— William Shakespeare

this princess of wales
whose kindness never failed
but alas life is no fairy tale
not even the royal are invincible
with the pictures the paparazzi took
she gave the world one last look
a noble heart so angelic & big
& now she is dead . . .

" I don't go by any rule book ...
I lead by the heart, not the head."
— Princess Diana

an unrivaled master of martial arts
at war with demons in the dark
he fought & fought until it all turned tragic
but here is where he enters the dragon
for he who conquers the ego shall never end . . .

" Now, water can flow or it can crash.
Be water, my friend. "
— Bruce Lee

breakfast at tiffany's
& lunch on a roman holiday
all this made her the queen
of hollywood's golden age
an introvert who played extroverts
but in diamonds & fancy dresses
she saw no real worth
for she preferred helping others
with humanitarian efforts
blessed with the heart of an unselfish mother . . .

" The best thing to hold onto in life is each other. "
— Audrey Hepburn

those chains of oppression
almost brought down a fractured nation
the south was fighting for a way of life
based on slaves & plantations
it seems with the declaration of independence
we did not learn our lesson
states' rights versus a union's might
& the final outcome was blood & aggression
but there was also his famous proclamation
for the tall bearded man in the stovetop hat
only wanted them to understand . . .

" A house divided against itself cannot stand. "
— Abraham Lincoln

here was a dreadlocked prophet
who knew that life wasn't bought with a profit
jamaican saint of the rasta faith
who sung his soul to cast out snakes
his music the cure for venomous hate
now
three little birds are perched on babylon's gate
they know that as long as his spirit is kept alive
his songs & his lyrics
will heal the ill & the blind . . .

" One love, one heart ...
let's get together and feel alright. "
— Bob Marley

there is no south american more hated & loved
from below or above
was he evil or good
devil or demigod
perhaps he was both
& that's why he remains a global icon
he arose from argentina with an ideological cause
then liberated cuba in a communist revolution
then spread rebellion from the congo to bolivia
until the cia finally had enough
his heart began to beat
but he stood perfectly still on his feet
a revolutionary until his last stand . . .

" I know you are here to kill me.
Shoot, coward,
you are only going to kill a man. "
— Che Guevara

lover of garden parties & perfumed wigs
a posing queen of the decadent
what she did not see was her biggest mistake
the total collapse of the royal french state
now a starving mob is storming the palace gates
& all because they thought she said . . .

" Let them eat cake. "
— Marie Antoinette

parliament almost became smoldering embers
remember remember the 5th of november
a pack of catholics with a gunpowder plot
wanted no part of protestant pomp
bonfires & fireworks now light up the streets
the monarchy's potential ruin a distant memory
but still his face lives on
a mask for every rebellious cause
a violent effigy . . .

" A desperate disease requires
a dangerous remedy. "
— Guy Fawkes

a village under the swirling moonlight
immortalized by his starry night
but hidden from the eye lies a troubled mind
he knows not why this lethal feeling
not even his wheat field crows can conceal it
for what all those lovely stars & sunflowers betray
is the darkness he could not paint away . . .

" I often think that the night is more alive
and more richly colored than the day. "
— Vincent van Gogh

mental midgets on carousels
& gigantic lizards playing slot machines
he stumbles around this crazy town
hallucinating the american dream
acid tabs & bat wings on a strange odyssey
drugs & white rabbits are telling him what to believe
a modern day alice in wonderland is what he'll write
entering this desert of neon light
filled with fear & with flight . . .

" Some may never live, but the crazy never die. "
– Hunter S. Thompson

he will open the doors of the universe
with piano keys
he will shake the foundations of the earth
with a symphony
behold this gift & this curse
composing the music of heavenly spheres
with hearing eyes & blind ears
what godlike sounds he wrought
as if the moonlight could sing & talk
beyond the holy & the damned
he creates beauty with immortal hands . . .

" Music should strike fire from the heart of man,
and bring tears from the eyes of woman. "
— Ludwig van Beethoven

blessed with the soul of a revolutionary
in mexico he became legendary
the rich had taken control of the land
ruling the poor with a cruel hand
thus the people needed his help
so out of the desert he rode like hell
with rows of bullets upon each belt
battle after battle he fought
outrunning the u.s. & the law
until the revolution was won
& he returned home to chihuahua
thinking that nothing could go wrong
but the powerful still saw him as a threat
& one day as the sun was setting
they sent a drunken assassin to kill him
there was no more running
deny your heroes & accept your kings . . .

" Don't let it end this way
tell them I said something. "
— Pancho Villa

a revolution in physics was born in his mind
equations that solved the mysteries of matter & light
energy & relativity explained with fabulous simplicity
theories that would make him
the most famous genius in history
those wild shocks of hair
a smoking pipe wafting in the air
sitting at a desk in his favorite gray sweater
& of course e=mc squared
the brilliance of the cosmos
contained in three little letters . . .

" Look deep in nature,
and then you will understand everything better. "
— Albert Einstein

he changed his name from cassius clay
then became an undisputed heavyweight
a fighter to the fullest degree
his war was here & not with the vietnamese
so he protested american foreign policy
with bold words & sharp fists he recites poetry
an immortal king of the boxing ring . . .

" Float like a butterfly and sting like a bee! "
— Muhammad Ali

the last queen of egypt
lover of antony & caesar
who met her final fate
with the kiss of a snake
golden nile at twilight
she stares at it one last time
dreams of empire left undone
there no more tears left to cry . . .

" All strange and terrible events are welcome,
but comforts we despise. "
— Cleopatra

the smoke in his lungs
more ominous than seattle clouds
this sad god of grunge
weaving together his magical sound
no i don't have a gun
were the lyrics in his song
so between sorrow & irony
is where he was caught
& shocked were the fates
when they heard that final shot. . .

" I'd rather be hated for who I am
than loved for who I am not. "
— Kurt Cobain

he sits under the bodhi tree
meditating on
all that is
all that was
& all that he must leave
enlightenment & bliss
suffering & death
this web of thoughts
that catches us
like egocentric spiders
& all because we're blinded
by attachment & desire
but everything that isn't us also reminds us
nothing in this universe remains divided
even life & death are secretly united
the rewards & torments of karma
forever turning & reborn
upon the wheel of samsara
but on this gentle evening
he is leaving for nirvana
he sits under the bodhi tree
meditating on
all that is
all that was
& all that he must leave . . .

" Even death is not to be feared
by one who lives wisely. "
— The Buddha

Made in the USA
Columbia, SC
20 August 2024

40277742R00039